BLACK BROWN & BEAUTIFULLY Me

BY: IZZIE WILSON

ACKOWLEDGEMENTS

TO EVERY BEAUTIFUL BLACK, BROWN & BEAUTIFUL CHILD; KNOW THAT YOU ARE ENOUGH, YOU ARE CAPABLE, AND YOUR MELANIN IS BEAUTIFUL. ALWAYS BE PROUD OF WHO YOU ARE AND NEVER LET ANYONE DIM YOUR LIGHT. I HOPE THAT AS YOU FLIP THROUGH THE PAGES OF THIS BOOK, YOU KNOW THAT YOUR BLACK AND BROWN SKIN IS BEAUTIFUL!

TO MY MOM; WHO HAS ALWAYS BELIEVED IN ME AND POURED INTO ME AFFIRMING ME IN EVERY WAY POSSIBLE. THANK YOU.

TO THE LITTLE GIRL THAT I WAS; I AM PROUD OF YOU. I AM PROUD OF WHO YOU WERE, ALL THAT YOU HAVE OVERCOME, WHO YOU ARE TODAY, AND ALL THAT YOU WILL BE.

ARTWORK CREATED THROUGH THE USE OF ARTIFICIAL INTELLIGENCE.

ABOUT THE AUTHOR
Izzie Wilson

Izzie Wilson, a high school senior, set out to create a meaningful senior project that would both leave a lasting impact, while reflecting on her K-12 experience. After reflection, Black, Brown, & Beautifully Me was born—a children's book designed to affirm and empower young Black and Brown children. Understanding that positive affirmations are critical in building confidence and a strong racial identity, Wilson sought to create a space where children can embrace their beauty, strength, and worth.

MY BLACK AND BROWN SKIN IS BEAUTIFUL.

MY CROWN IS A GIFT.

IT ELEVATES ME, ANCHORS MY PRIDE, AND LIFTS ME FAR AND WIDE.

FEARLESS LIKE MALCOLM X AND **TRUE** LIKE BARACK OBAMA...

I'M **CHANGING** THE VIEW!

MY MELANIN IS A MASTERPIECE... WORTH CELEBRATING, HONORING, AND LOVING.

MY MIND IS A UNIVERSE FULL OF ENDLESS POSSIBILITIES.

THERE IS NO ONE WITH MY MIND—
I'M ONE OF A KIND!

I AM STRONG, I AM FREE, UNIQUE, AND PROUD OF ALL THAT MAKES ME, ME!

I LOVE MY BLACK, BROWN, AND BEAUTIFUL SKIN.

MY SKIN IS DEEP AND TRUE.
IT MAKES THE PERFECT HUE.

I AM BLACK, BROWN, AND OH SO BEAUTIFULLY ME!

Made in the USA
Columbia, SC
17 March 2025